Fearchair

THE RO ...NE
WANDERER

HIS LIFE AND SAYINGS

BY
THE AUTHOR OF "THE MAID OF FAIRBURN,"
&c., &c.

Third Edition—Revised and Enlarged

CONTENTS

British Library Cataloguing in Publication Data
A catalogue record for this book is available from the British Library.
ISBN 1-899863-02-8

© 1995 House of Lochar

The 1908 edition of *Fearchair-a-Ghunna* was
published by Eneas MacKay, Stirling

Printed in Great Britain by SRP Ltd, Exeter
for House of Lochar, Isle of Colonsay, Argyll PA61 7YP

FEARCHAIR-A-GHUNNA,

THE ROSS-SHIRE WANDERER.

CHAPTER I.—Early Life.

Birthplace — Education — Personal Appearance — Incipient Eccentricity—Story of Early Life—Smuggling—Burning the Gauger's Cottage — His Brother's Death — Punishing the Informer—Adrift.

FARQUHAR MACLENNAN, *alias* Fearchair-a-Ghunna, was born in Strathconon, Ross-shire, in the year 1784, and spent his youth in that district. Little is known regarding his life during that period, and probably it was as uneventful as were the lives of his neighbours in the beautiful strath mentioned. His father, a well-to-do crofter as crofters went, did not think it necessary to burden his children with a school education, and even had the idea occurred to him there were but few facilities for carrying it out. Poor Farquhar was therefore so destitute of literary attainments that, to the day of his death, he could not distinguish A from B. His knowledge of the English language was also very limited, the only words he assayed being "yes" and "no." But though thus unlearned

A

and unaccomplished, young Farquhar received the elements of a more practical education on the farm and on the moor. Shooting, smuggling, and agriculture appear to have been the three principal pursuits of the district in those times, and in the first two of these the subject of this sketch took great delight.

Farquhar's personal appearance was quite in keeping with his character and mode of life. He was somewhat low in stature, but firmly built, with broad square shoulders, and at this period possessed a gait remarkably erect and almost stately. His head was covered with a profusion of long, bristly hair, which seldom, if ever, was combed. His eyes were small, restless, and piercing, while a fixed determination was stamped on his care-worn countenance.

It is not now known whether in his early youth Farquhar was subject to that aberration of intellect which, in later years, caused him to take to a wandering life. The probability is that it was of gradual growth, though its progress was eventually hastened by the troubles resulting from the smuggling propensities of the family. There is one story told of Farquhar's youth which indicates that he had begun even thus early to show symptoms of mental disease or eccentricity.

It was in the spring season of the year that Farquhar's father, who had no grain-seed for his croft, sent him for a supply of seed to Strathpeffer, which was famed for the purity of its

barley. A journey from Strathconon to Strathpeffer at the time in question was no easy task,
for the road between those places was then
quite different from the one now there. However, Farquhar at length reached his destination,
got the barley, put it on his back, and returned
home. He arrived at Strathconon about mid-
night, and, finding that his father had retired
to bed, he set to work and sowed the barley.
Although the people of Strathconon were not
early risers, their fowls were, and every hen,
chicken, and cock, within reach of Farquhar's
newly-sown barley, were picking it up for hours
ere a single person in the Strath had got up.
It was towards evening when Farquhar told
that he had sown the barley, and by that time
almost every grain of it had been picked off the
ground. When his father chided him for having
sown the barley during the night, he readily
replied—"*Esan aig am bitheadh barr math
agus foghar luathrach féumaidh e bhi moch-
thra. Am bitheadh tu air eiridh tratha 'sa
mhaduinn agus an talamh a bhi air a cliathadh,
cha'n itheadh na h-eoin an t-sil,*" *i.e.,* "He who
would have a good crop and an early harvest
must be up betimes. Had you risen in time
in the morning, and harrowed the ground, the
fowls could not have eaten the seed." For
this answer his father gave him such a severe
castigation that it is supposed to have
injuriously affected his naturally feeble mind.
    Another and a different story told of one of

the causes that led to the weakness of intellect
he displayed belongs to this period. We give
it as related by a Redcastle neighbour of our
hero. When a lad, Fearchair was engaged as
a herd by a Ferintosh farmer. His master was
a man very exacting in his demands for early
rising on the part of his servants ; he could not
get enough of work out of them. At break of
day he was rousing them up. Fearchair and
the ploughman resolved to play a trick on their
employer, and one night, in the harvest time,
they cut a lot of divots and built up his bedroom
window so as to totally exclude the chance of
daylight penetrating. The farmer got up several
times during the early morning, and as often
retired to bed, as the daylight had not appeared.
At last he began to suspect a trick had been
played on him, and, dressing himself, went to
the door, when the mid-day sun shone upon
him. He then examined the window, and,
discovering the cause of the darkness, he was
greatly enraged. He rushed into the farmyard
and seized a spade ; the first person he met was
Fearchair, and, lifting the weapon, he struck
him on the top of the head with the flat side.
It is said that from that time Farquhar's weakness of understanding became more marked.

Fearchair seems to have been remarkably
unfortunate in his engagements when a youth.
After leaving the service of this Ferintosh
farmer, he engaged as a herd with a man
named Gray, at Croftruny, in the parish of

Redcastle. While tending his charge one warm day in summer, he lay down on the soft grass, and, as herds frequently do, fell asleep. The consequence was that his cattle, one after another, went into a cornfield close by. Gray noticed the cattle in the corn, and, after driving them out of it, found poor Fearchair in the land of dreams, and without making any attempt to awaken him, struck him a blow on the side of the head with a spade he was carrying at the time. The blow broke the sleeper's collar-bone and made an ugly gash in the upper part of his cheek, the scar of which he carried while he lived.

About eighty years ago, smuggling was carried on extensively in all parts of the Highlands and Islands of Scotland, but in no part, it is said, did it attain to such a height as in Strathconon, where it entirely superseded every lawful branch of industry. It proved a curse rather than a blessing to the quiet inhabitants of the Strath, profiting none but ruining many. The Strathconon smugglers, like their neighbours, the smugglers of Strathcarron, transacted most of their business with the citizens of Inverness, whither they always went during the night; and many a bloody encounter took place between themselves and the Excise Officers, the latter generally coming off second best. Ultimately the fame of Strathconon as a place of illicit distillation had spread far and wide, and the Board of Excise resolved to station a staff of Officers in the district in order, if possible, to put a stop to the illegal trade. A cottage near the scene of operations was procured and put into order for the reception of the Exciseman and his staff, but when the repairs were all but completed, the cottage, which was thatched with heather, was found one morning a heap of ashes, it having been burnt during the night. That this was the work of an incendiary there was no doubt whatever; and every person in the Strath knew that Farquhar had something to do with it, though no one could be induced to divulge the fact. The Excise Officers were most zealous in their efforts to discover the guilty party, but they were completely foiled in their endeavours. Farquhar, being known as a leading smuggler, was apprehended on suspicion and brought to Dingwall, but, although he was subjected to a most searching examination on the way thither, nothing was elicited from him. At Dingwall various schemes of examining him were adopted with the view of extorting anything he might know regarding the burning of the cottage, but to no purpose; he was as mute as a lamb, and gazed at his inquisitors unconcernedly, who were consequently forced to release him. The Excise Officers were armed with cutlasses in those days, and in order to extort a confession from Farquhar the Exciseman of the district declared that he would cut off his head unless he gave the desired information. "*Faodaidh tu fhaighinn bho mo cheann na's urrainn duit, ach cha'n fhaigh thu ni sam bith bhuam-sa*," said Fearchair; *i.e.*, "You may get all the information from my head that you can, but you will get none from me." Notwithstanding the vigilance of the Excise Officers placed in the glen, smuggling was still carried on in Strathconon, and one of the most notorious defenders was a brother of Farquhar Maclennan. This individual was one of the strongest men in the Strath—there were some herculeans in Strathconon in those days—but in an encounter with the gaugers he was accidentally killed. This circumstance excited Farquhar to an extraordinary degree, and he vowed he would be revenged for the death of his brother, whom he loved intensely. It is said that he watched by day and night for an opportunity to kill the man whom he regarded as his brother's murderer, but he does not seem to have got that opportunity. From that time, however, Farquhar Maclennan was a changed man.

The smuggling troubles of the Maclennan family, however, were not yet over. A treacherous neighbour betrayed to the Excise Officers the site of their illicit distillery, and one dark night old Maclennan was caught red-handed at the illegal work. He was taken to Dingwall and heavily fined, while the implements and produce found on the spot were confiscated. In his rage at this untoward

event, Farquhar was easily prevailed on by
his comrades to revenge himself on the
informer by setting fire to his house and
steading.

It is said that Farquhar's imbecility was
at this time feigned to screen him from the
consequence of his offence, but we have seen
that on a former occasion he showed signs of
derangement. The truth seems to be that
these accumulating troubles all combined to
cloud his spirit. He now began to think that
he was marked out for some dread judgment,
and ultimately he gave way to his terrors.
Without informing anyone of his intention, he
wandered out into the world to search for the
peace of mind which he could not obtain on
the banks of the Conon. Farquhar was
twenty-five years of age when, one fine day
towards the end of the spring of 1809, he
turned his back on the home of his childhood.
He never returned to it again or expressed a
longing to see it, until he neared the end of
his earthly pilgrimage, and then he merely
asked that his body should be laid with the
dust of his forefathers in the old churchyard
at Strathconon. Yet he never forgot his home
and kindred, nor showed any shame for the
records of his family. When asked from
whom he was descended, he always replied
readily and proudly — " *Ghineadh mi bho
Poitearan Srath-chonain*," meaning, " I am
sprung from the Smugglers of Strathconon."

CHAPTER II.—The Wanderer.

A Vagabond Life—Farquhar's Dress—Accoutrements—Gun—
Gatherings — Mode of Travelling — Kessock Ferry — The
Railway — Keen Scent — Disturbing the Congregation —
Fearchair v. Minister—Culloden—Fairburn—Kilcoy.

A wandering life in the Highlands during
the first half of this century was a very different
thing from modern vagrancy. The Highland
rover in old times was generally a more or less
interesting object, and in the absence of poor
laws he could generally count on an hospitable
reception. Some of the wanderers, of whom
Farquhar was one, declined to be classed with
common beggars, but, on the contrary, set up
as gentlemen-at-large to entertain whom
should not be considered a trouble, but an
honour.

When Farquhar had bidden farewell to Strathconon, he travelled for some time through
various parts of Ross-shire, where he neither
worked nor lacked, but ultimately he began to
confine his tours to the Black Isle and the
opposite shores of the Beauly Firth. Throughout that district he soon became a general
favourite especially among the young folk, and

never was in want of food or tobacco, the
latter being the only luxury for which he
showed a fondness.

Farquhar's dress was so fantastic that a
description of it must be given. He wore a
blue Kilmarnock bonnet, replaced in his later
years by a wide-awake hat, but it would often
be difficult to say what was the shape or
character of his head-gear, so completely
hidden would it be under the profusion of
feathers, bits of paper, and other ornaments
which he stuck thereon. A substantial iron
chain fastened under the chin kept the head-
dress in position. His clothes were generally
of various bright colours and secured by
another heavy chain, or iron-wire girdle passing
round his body. In his wanderings he picked
up all the pieces of old metal, bones, rags,
paper, and feathers he came across, which he
pinned or tied to his clothing and carried
about with him for weeks; and, when
thoroughly covered with these decorations, he
resembled a large bundle of rags and filthy
matter, rather than a human being.

But the other parts of his outfit were no less
extraordinary. The burden of flotsam and
jetsam which he generally carried was firmly
bound on his shoulders with numerous chains.
A brace of cast-away pistols hung at his iron
belt, also a Mexican powder-horn, several iron
hoops, pieces of chain, and a bunch of keys.
During one part of his career an old sword was

added to his other accoutrements, but it disappeared, probably because it was too good for daily wear.

The great characteristic feature of Farquhar's equipment, however, was his gun. He had an over-weening fondness for guns, and was never without one—hence the appellation of Fearchair-a-Ghunna, "Farquhar of the Gun," by which he was generally known. Usually Farquhar's gun was of the most wonderful construction. During the earlier period of his wandering life he carried over half-a-dozen old gun barrels, which were tied together with a string or chain in such a way that they resembled a rude, monster revolver, the stock of which he himself formed out of the thick end of a tree, and was about as heavy as a man could lift off the ground. Even Farquhar found it too heavy to use at the shoulder, and so he got a rest made for it. He also carried a pan with a burning peat to fire the powder. The operation in firing was first to get the gun adjusted on the rest to the requisite level, then to lay a train of powder to each of the six barrels, and lastly to apply the peat. The six barrels went off simultaneously, causing a tremendous report, but seldom, if ever, doing anything serious. From the following incident it may be surmised that Fearchair himself in his secret soul felt that his weapon was not so useful as a simpler gun might be. One day he met the Redcastle gamekeeper,

who was carrying a beautiful single-barrelled
gun on his shoulder. Fearchair, who expressed
a desire to see his gun, was at once gratified,
and after examining it carefully, proposed that
they might, with advantage, make an exchange.
"*Bhiodh mo ghunna, ars esa glé shoirbheachail
dhutsa. Bhiodh agad sia gunnachan an aitena
h-aon, agus de'n upraid dheanamh sin am
measg nan eun,*" said Fearchair; *i.e.*, "My
gun would be of immense service to you.
You should have six guns instead of one,
and what havoc that would do among
the moor fowls!" We need hardly say
that the keeper declined to strike a bargain
with him. The gun which Fearchair carried
in his later years was of the most unique
description—an old rusty barrel without either
lock or stock. There were, however, some
changes in his mode of handling it. As soon
as he saw a crow near the roadside he would
take aim, and holding the gun thus, his next
proceeding was to light a match and apply it
to the touch-hole.

Fearchair was a great collector of all sorts of
articles, and nothing came amiss for his
burden. Things that were thrown away as
worthless were collected by him and stored
in his house. For some of these articles he
found a ready market in Inverness, and
accordingly he paid periodic visits to that
town to sell his wares, but a great part of
them consisted of the merest rubbish, and

these were hoarded up with miserly care. This was particularly the case with pretty stones which he picked up on his travels, and of which several cart loads were found in his house after his demise. It should be added that his burden very generally contained a dead fowl or rabbit found by the wayside.

Farquhar's load would often be more than sufficient for a donkey, but he always trudged along on foot, seldom trusting himself to any other mode of locomotion, and though cumbered with his goods to such an extent that it really seemed a wonder how he could move at all, the wanderer travelled, and even danced, with an agility that was truly amazing. On reaching Beauly on his way to Inverness with a burden of goods one fine summer day, he was met by some of the crew of a vessel which was about to leave for Inverness. The day being warm and his load heavy, they prevailed on him to take a passage in the vessel. Shortly after he had stepped on board, and when the vessel was just loosing from the wharf, he overheard some of the crew saying that they were bound for Newcastle. This was only a ruse to frighten him, but he had scarcely heard it when he cleared the ship's bulwarks and the open space betwixt the vessel and the quay at a bound, with his burden and all. As soon as he got on *terra firma*, Fearchair, in unmeasured terms, denounced the sailors for attempting to carry

him away, and even declared that if he had
it in his power he would send them to the
bottom.

The Ross-shire Wanderer was so attached
to his burden that though it were ever so
heavy it was utterly impossible to induce him
to lay it off his back—even when resting, or
when crossing Kessock Ferry, as the following
anecdote will show. He was passing East
High Street, Inverness, one day with a heavy
burden of his customary ware, and when
opposite a woollen and yarn warehouse, immediately to the east of the Market Brae,
he was accosted by an acquaintance, who
asked him if he had come across Kessock
Ferry. " *Cha d'thainig ars' an fhogarach.
Tha na Fir-aiseig cho neoach cha toil leo
mise fhaicinn le m'uallach a' dol stigh do'n
a bhata aca, agus, na's mo, tha mi air mo
chràthàdh aig an aiseag leis na luchd cuairt
gu'm bheil mi air mo ghranachadh gabhail
an rathaid sin. Thainig, mi mu'n cuairt
Manachainn 'Ic Shimidh—ach oh ! dhuine,
ciod de h-urrad do chloimh a tha an sin
(omharrach adh an taigh-thasgaidh). Nach
e bhiodh breagh air son dlùth ?*" i.e., " No,
I have not. These ferrymen are so peculiar
that they don't care to see me going into their
boat with my bundle, and, besides, I am so
tormented at the Ferry by passengers and
others that I am disgusted to go that way.
I came round by Beauly—but oh ! man, what

a lot of yarn is there (pointing to the warehouse). It would be grand for wafts and warps!"

Fearchair was an old man before the railway was introduced into the district, and he never travelled by it. He was once, however, on the point of doing so, but the result of the attempt was not of a kind to induce him to try it again. When Fearchair was in Inverness selling his goods some time after the opening of the Ross-shire line, a certain wag, with whom he was acquainted, met him on the street, and advised him to go to the station and take the train for Tarradale. Fearchair, however, hesitated, but at length consented; and, going to the station, took his seat in one of the carriages of the north-going train, but was hardly seated when the ticket collector came round and demanded his ticket. Poor Fearchair, who had nothing of the kind (for his adviser had meanly omitted to supply him with one), was ruthlessly dragged out of the carriage, and left sprawling on the platform. As soon as he recovered his equilibrium, he grinned and said—" *Tha an rathaid so cuimhneachadh dhomh Bord an Tighearn cha'n eil a h-aon air an ceadachadh a' ghabhail mur eil comharradh aige,*" *i.e.* "This road reminds me of the Lord's Table—no one being permitted to take it, unless he is provided with a token or ticket."

During a long period of his wanderings in the Black Isle, Fearchair was accommodated,

when so disposed, in an out-house belonging to
the Manse at Redcastle. While in possession
of this out-house, which he had filled up with
stones, metal, bones, rags, iron, old shoes, rooks,
and frogs (and wherever he took up his abode he
always amassed a store of these articles, which
completely filled up the interior until there was
scarcely room enough left for him to turn about
in), the minister, the Rev. Mr. Macrae, who
had been settled there after the Disruption,
peeped one day into Fearchair's dwelling, and
said :— "*Fuigh ! fuigh ! 's ann agad tha 'm
faileadh Fhearchair,*" *i.e.*, "Faugh! faugh! you
have a very bad smell, Farquhar." Fearchair
answered :—" *Tha iad 'g innseadh dhomhsa
gum bheil faileadh maith aig na feidh, ach
tha faileadh ni's fearr agadsa, 'nuair a fhuair
thu faileadh stiopain a' Chaisteil-Ruaidh 'n
America,*" *i.e.*, "They tell me that the deer
have a keen scent ; but you have keener,
when you scented the Redcastle stipend from
America," another rendering being :—" *Tha
iad ag innseadh dhomhsa gu'm bheil cuinnlein
glan aig na feidh, ach 's ann agadsa bha na
cuinnlein glan 'nuair a fhuair thu faileadh
stiopain a' Chaisteil-Ruaidh 'n America.*"
The gentleman in question had come from
America to fill up the vacant charge, and
hence Fearchair's cutting answer.

Being asked one day shortly after the
vacancy caused by the Disruption had been
filled up at Killearnan, why he did not attend

the Established Church there as formerly, he gave a peculiar look to his interrogator, and replied significantly:—"*Tha imcheist orm a dol do'n eaglais sin suas, oir nan rachainn bhiodh an coimhthional uile (nach eil, tha e air innseadh dhomhsa, na's motha ann an aireamh nan ordagan mo chois chearr) gun chomas coimhead rium. Chailleadh iad, uime sin, an t-sochair dheth an t-searmon deas-bhriathrach agus druidhteach a bhiodh air a labhairt leis a mhinisteir cliuteach agus sron-geur-'ach,*" or, "I refrain from going to that church now, because if I did go the *whole* congregation (which don't, I am told, outnumber the toes of my left foot) could not help looking at me. They would, therefore, lose the benefit of the eloquent and impressive sermon preached by the worthy and esteemed keen-nosed clergyman."

In the above answer, Fearchair sharpened his arrow and shot it with a vengeance.

One day he took it into his head that some of the domestics of the manse had, during his absence, tampered with his goods, and, determined to be revenged, he retaliated by stealing the plough irons and destroying the minister's potatoes. The latter he accomplished by making holes with his staff in the roofs of the potato pits, and then carried salt-water from the sea and poured it into the holes thus made until the pits were flooded. It need scarcely be said that the potatoes were completely destroyed. For this offence Fearchair was apprehended and brought before the Sheriff at Dingwall, but he was immediately discharged, as the proof against him was insufficient. It is related that when the Sheriff asked him why he did it, Fearchair answered—"*Ma ta, a Shiorramh, nach d' thoireadh tu peanas air an duine a mhilleadh do leabhraichean agus paipearan?*"—"Well, Sheriff, would you not punish the man that would destroy your books and papers?" On returning to Killearnan after the trial, Fearchair met the minister, and told him that he had lived at Redcastle before him, and that he would probably do so after him, adding—"*Bheirinn comhairle dhuit Mhr Macrath deagh aire thoirt dhuit fhein*"— "I would advise you, Mr. Macrae, to take good care of yourself." This remark was substantiated, for Fearchair was sometimes at Redcastle many years after the clergyman had left it.

The Rev. Mr. Macrae had a favourite Newfoundland dog, which died under peculiar circumstances, and on being dissected the lungs of the animal were found pierced with upwards of a hundred pins. It would appear that Fearchair had administered to the dog a doze consisting of leaven filled with pins. This conduct the minister could not stand, and one day while Fearchair was absent he ordered several men to have the whole contents of Fearchair's domicile removed and cast into the sea. When Fearchair returned, and found that his goods (which to him were precious) were gone, his rage knew no bounds, and he left the place, declaring that he would be revenged on the minister. This threat he carried out by stealing everything left unsecured about the premises, and tossing it into the sea.

While serving a Ferintosh farmer, Fearchair ascertained that that property belonged to Mr. Forbes of Culloden; and in acknowledgment of the kind treatment he received on that estate, he went periodically to Culloden House to pay, as he used to say, his "respects to the good proprietor." Fearchair's visits to Culloden were always longed for and appreciated by the servants, to whom his uncouth appearance with his load of rags and iron afforded great amusement; and not less so did his curt answers to all their queries as he sat on a form beside the massive table in the kitchen, his keen eyes watching their every movement.

Fearchair also frequently visited Fairburn House, and he was never allowed to go away without first receiving a good meal. It happened on one occasion that the cook coaxed him to take more food than was good for him, and the result was that he soon became uncomfortable, and at length ran out to the lawn, where he began to roll himself on the grass in great agony, exclaiming vociferously, " *O thig Tighearna uile chaomh agus cuir ceann air mo*

*bheatha truagh oir tha mi ann an pian uam-
hasach,*" *i.e.*, "Lord God Almighty, put an end
at once to my miserable life, for I am in dread-
ful pain." He then began to abuse the cook
in good round terms for having given him so
much of her good things, and declared that he
would be avenged for what she had done.

The Wanderer frequently visited the house
of a farmer in the heights of Kilcoy, who
successfully carried on the same trade
which Fearchair followed in his earlier years,
namely, smuggling. On the occasion of these
visits, he always received as much of John
Barleycorn as he liked to take, and invariably
finished off with a dance. As he never laid
down his burden, this performance afforded
the greatest possible sport to the scores of
young people who assembled there for the
express purpose of seeing him dance. He
would continue the exercise for about an hour,
his chains and hoops supplying the music.

Like many other weak-minded persons, poor
Fearchair was sometimes imposed upon by
unprincipled persons. After a round through
the Aird, and a call at Beaufort Castle, he
came one evening to Beauly with a heavy load
of goods on his back, and his purse pretty well
replenished. On reaching the village, he called
at a shop and made some little purchases, and
then left for Tarradale, but had not been long
away from the shop when he returned, and told
the merchant that he was accosted by two men

near the Muir of Ord market stance, who robbed him of his purse and its contents. When Fearchair described the robbers, the merchant had no difficulty in recognising them as two drunken characters who were in his shop when Fearchair made his purchases, and had evidently observed where he had put his purse, otherwise they would have had no small difficulty in finding its *locus*, for Fearchair was always so well padded with his heterogeneous burden that it would take all the skill of a Scotland Yard detective to find a particular article. The thieves were strangers in the district, and the merchant did not think it worth while to set the police on their track— he thought they would be sufficiently punished if one half of Fearchair's anathemas fell upon them, for the Wanderer earnestly implored Heaven not to let them pass unpunished.

CHAPTER III.—Eccentricities.

" The Garrison "—Food—The Major's Dog—Gunpowder—
Shooting Incident—The Strike Fire—Shooting Accidents—
Hunting a Donkey—Stone Blasting—"Guard your Life"—In
Beauly Ferry—"Smoking" the Rooks.

Fearchair-a-Ghunna was full of whims and
oddities, and though generally able to take care
of himself, he seemed incapable of doing anything like other people. We have already seen
how eccentric he was in regard to clothing and
personal habits, and his views on dwellings were
no less extraordinary. After being ejected from
the minister's out-house at Redcastle, Fearchair
went to the Muir of Tarradale, where he found
an old deserted hut of which he took possession.
It was of the most primitive construction; the
walls, which were formed of boulders and sods,
were low and thick; the roof was thatched with
broom, brackens, and heather, and the interior
consisted of one apartment. This tenement
Fearchair proceeded to furnish in accordance
with his own notions, but the greater part of it
was occupied by his accumulating rubbish.
He named it the " Garrison," and was at great
pains to protect it against burglars. At one

time he was somewhat indisposed, and, thinking that he was about to die, set to and built up the door of this house with stones so as to make it a tomb, stating that it was his desire to have his body left in the "Garrison" till the day of judgment. Before he died, however, he expressed a different wish.

In regard to food, Fearchair was anything but fastidious. He often ate the bodies of fowls and rabbits raw, which he devoured greedily; and sometimes, though a house were quite near at hand, he preferred to light a fire in the open air and roast parts of grouse and rooks which had died from disease or otherwise, and been picked up by the way. He even liked to eat frogs; but he made it a point to take out their eyes, as he did not like to see them looking so steadfastly at him while he was devouring them. It need hardly be said that this food was anything but wholesome, more especially as it was neither cleaned nor properly dressed. He called a ditch that passed through a certain marshy place in the parish of Redcastle, "the red herring fishing grounds," on account of the large number of frogs that existed in it.

It is said that Fearchair's unscrupulous voracity sometimes made him acquainted with strange companions, and the following story is in point. There lived in Ross-shire a certain Major for whom Fearchair entertained no great favour. It happened on one occasion that an old horse lay dead in the neighbourhood of the Major's residence, and Fearchair went for a piece of the carcase. On reaching it, he found the Major's dog helping himself to a good repast, and Fearchair at once began to help himself too; but immediately he commenced, the dog began to growl. "*'S ann ort tha drein a Mhaidseir*," said Fearchair, "*Cum do'n taobh agad fhein, cuiridh mise sreath eadarinn, cha teid mise seachad air, agus tha dochas agam nach tig thusa thairis air mar an ceudna*," the meaning of which is, "The Major's snarl is on your face." "Keep to your own side man," Fearchair continued, addressing the dog, "I will put a line between us (drawing a line on the carcase), I won't pass it, and I hope you won't come over it either."

Fearchair had a particular fondness for gunpowder, in fact, there was nothing else that he loved so well. He often said that, next to his Creator, there was no object that he venerated so much, and he would visit all the gamekeepers' houses for miles around for a supply of the coveted article. This fondness was very likely formed in his old poaching days in Strathconon, but it continued strong, even when the frailties of age rendered its gratification difficult. We have already seen how largely his shooting appliances bulked on his attention, and he took an extraordinary pleasure in using them. But with weapons so cumbrous, it is not surprising that Fearchair could kill nothing. His own opinion, however, was that he was a first-class shot, and if he fired at anything it must certainly be killed. One incident out of a hundred will illustrate this. He was rambling one day in the neighbourhood of Brahan Castle, and happening to see a crow close to him, he fired at it. On hearing the report of the gun, the crow, of course, flew away as merry and hale as ever. About a month afterwards, Fearchair was strolling near Redcastle—miles away from the scene of this exploit—and finding a dead crow which had been shot by some of the gamekeepers, he picked it up exclaiming : " *Seall so ! seall so ! so dealbh an rocais air an do loisg mi aig Caisteal Bhrahain. Dh-amais mi gu maith, agus b'fhiosrach dhomh gun do mharbh mi e, ged nach b'urrainn domh fhaotainn,*" *i.e.,* "Look here! look here! this is the very crow that I shot at Brahan Castle. I aimed well, and I knew I had killed it, though I could not find it." He cooked the crow in the open air and ate it !

As has been already remarked, Fearchair carried about with him a vessel containing a burning peat for the purpose of firing his gun, for lucifer matches were unknown during the earlier part of his wandering life, and his gun was not suited for any other means of igniting the powder. One day he went to a blacksmith's shop and told the blacksmith, whose name was Vulcan, that he sometimes lost good chances of shooting crows on account of the fire in his peat being extinguished by rain, or from other causes, and asked him whether he could invent something that would answer his purpose instead of the peat. The blacksmith answered that he could easily invent an instrument, and that he would make it and give it to him ere he left the shop if he would first say his peculiar prayer — *Urnuigh-na-Creubhaig*. Fearchair readily agreed, and repeated this remarkable prayer, the Gaelic and English version of which will be found in Chapter VII. of this sketch. When Fearchair had finished his prayer, the blacksmith began and soon formed a piece of steel to suit Fearchair's wrist, on which it was securely tied with a strong leathern thong. Vulcan then instructed him how to strike a piece of flint against the steel when he wanted a light. This piece of steel was never removed from Fearchair's wrist, either by day or by night, until he became ill.

Some of Fearchair's sporting experiences were not of a very pleasant kind. On one occasion he met with a rather severe accident when at a wild duck hunt. Having charged his six-barrelled gun, he proceeded to a part of the beach near Redcastle which he knew to be frequented by a number of wild ducks, and after lying on the shore for some time a few ducks came within range. He fired, and the next instant he was lying senseless on the shore. One or two of the barrels being overcharged had burst, and some of the pieces striking Fearchair on the head and face, cut him dreadfully. How long he lay insensible on the shore he did not know, but although he lost a large quantity of blood he soon recovered. Fearchair's gun seems to have had a penchant for bursting, for on another occasion when passing a field where a man was ploughing with a pair of horses, he noticed a crow, and fired at it; but, from some unaccountable cause, the gun burst, and flew in pieces through the air. One piece of the barrel struck the ground close to the ploughman's feet, and a bystander asked Fearchair how his gun had burst, pointing out that he had nearly killed a man. "Oh," said Fearchair, " *Bha an duine glice gu leoir cumail as an rathad. Dh-aithnich e nach b'urrainn na musgaidean sin earbsa. Cha d'rinn mi h-aon riamh, agus ma thachras doibh briseadh, cha'n eil mise ri choireachadh,*" or, "Oh! the man knew that these old muskets could not be trusted, and was wise enough to keep out of the way. I never made one, and if they chance to break I am not·to blame."

On one of his rounds he called one day at the mill of S——, and the miller, a jocular sort of fellow, addressing him, said:—"I don't see what is the use of you going about with that lockless musket, Fearchair. I will allow you to kill my dog, man, if you can." "*An cum thu dhomh e?*" *i.e.*, "Will you hold him (the dog) for me?" asked Fearchair eagerly. "I will, in-

deed," answered the miller, as he seized the dog
and held it for Fearchair to fire at. Fearchair
at once levelled his musket at the animal, and
began to blow the fire in the peat, which he
kept close to the priming. The explosion at
length took place, and several pieces of the pot-
metal, with which the musket was charged,
penetrated the ground at the miller's feet,
frightening him almost out of his wits, while one
metal splinter struck the dog's back, tearing off
a piece of the skin and flesh. The poor animal,
as might be expected, ran frantically away,
howling madly with pain and fear, to the no
small amusement of the subject of our sketch.
The miller candidly acknowledged that he had
acted very foolishly, and declared that had he
known that the musket contained any other
thing than powder, he would not for the world
have done what he did.

Fearchair was passing along a road at the
base of a hill on one occasion, and noticing
some quadruped browsing a little distance up
the hill, at once charged his gun, and cautiously
approached the animal until he got within a
reasonable distance of it, when he applied the
match in his usual way, and bang went the shot.
The quadruped, of course, was not touched, but,
on hearing the loud report of the gun, was
frightened and ran away, and thinking that
he had wounded the animal, Fearchair gave
chase for the purpose of bagging his game.
The harder Fearchair ran, however, the swifter

ran the animal, and for a whole day Fearchair continued chasing the animal. At length the latter, very much fatigued, made for a house in the valley, with Fearchair close at its heels. "Hallo," cried the occupier of the house, on seeing Fearchair running after the beast, "Why are you running after my ass, Fearchair?" "*Se th' am damh a thilg mi air a mhonadh, agus tha mi ruith na dheigh fad an latha,*" *i.e.*, "It's a stag that I shot on the hill, and I have been running after him the whole day." It was some time before the man could convince Fearchair that he was really chasing an ass instead of a stag. The Ross-shire Wanderer had never seen an ass before.

Fearchair-a-Ghunna had another way of using his beloved powder, and one which yielded him scarcely inferior pleasure. He spent much of his time in blasting stones for the Black Isle farmers, not for fee or reward, but merely on account of the childish delight he took in seeing and hearing the explosion when the powder was fired. It was most amusing to see this eccentric blaster at work. As soon as the match was applied to the fuse, he gave in stentorian tones the usual word of alarm—"Fire!" This he repeated several times, all the while running round the stone as hard as he could, and gradually enlarging the circle until the explosion took place.

Fearchair's simplicity, as well as his characteristic love for powder, are illustrated by the following authenticated anecdote. He was one day at the Muir of Ord market, where he saw two Ross-shire proprietors with whom he was well acquainted. Later in the day, noticing that they were joined by another gentleman whom he did not know, Fearchair dogged them for some little time, and when they separated for a moment he stepped up to one of the gentlemen with whom he was acquainted, and told him that he required some powder, and wished to ask their friend for some, but as the latter had no Gaelic, he was at a loss how to ask for it. "Go right up to him," said the Ross-shire proprietor, "present your gun to him, and say, 'Guard your life,' and he will give you as much powder as you like." Fearchair at once went up to the stranger, who was an English gentleman, presented his gun, and in his usual gruff manner, said:—"Guard your life." The gentleman received such a fright that he at once left the market, and although both the Ross-shire gentlemen assured him that Fear- chair had no bad intention, they themselves having put the words in his mouth, they could not persuade him to stay.

One day Fearchair was returning home from Inverness, and, wishing to shorten his journey, went to Beauly ferry and asked two youths whom he found at the boat to ferry him across. They told him they would do so if he would first repeat *Urnuigh-na-Creubhaig*, but he was so disgusted, as already mentioned, by people asking him to say his prayer, that he refused them point blank. The youths, being as obstinate as Fearchair himself, kept him standing at the water's edge for a considerable time. At length, however, a party came to the ferry, who, being in haste, at once leaped into the boat, and although heavy laden with his wares, Fearchair jumped into the boat as nimbly as any of the others, and was at once rowed across. Immediately on her bow touching the beach, the other passengers sprang out of the boat, and were hastening towards the village long ere Fearchair thought of leaving his seat, and as soon as they had left the youths rowed out to the centre of the stream, notwithstanding Fearchair's remonstrances with them to the contrary. Finding that his appeals to be allowed ashore were disregarded, he sprang into the water, and, notwithstanding his heavy load of iron, his rags and cloak floated him like a buoy. When his feet touched the ground on the Inverness side of the ferry he exclaimed, "Had I known that the ground was so near me I would have left your rotten craft long ago, you wicked vagabonds, *Mo mhallachd oirbh*," that is, "My curse rest on you."

In the wood of Ardochy, parish of Urray, there was a rookery, and one day, when Fearchair was in the height of his strength, he took it into his head that if he could smoke the rooks out in much the same way as is done to bees, he could have flesh sufficient to last him for twelve months. With this strange idea in his head, and having everything prepared, he went to the rookery one evening when it was dark, so that the rooks would not see him, and windy so that they would not hear, but when crossing the bridge of Orrin on his way to Ardochy, he was met by a boy from near Tarradale, whom Fearchair had nick-named "Nossing" (Nothing), on account of the manner in which he used to tease the Wanderer. "Is that you, Fearchair?" asked the boy when they met. "Yes, that is my name," answered Fearchair, "are you Mr Nossing?" The boy replied in the affirmative, and they both sat down to rest at the end of the bridge. On "Nossing" learning where the other was going, he asked him for a penny worth of shot, at the same time showing Fearchair the penny. "Nossing" got a few grains of shot, and, offering Fearchair a bit of stone in payment, ran off as fast as he could, but had scarcely sat down in his father's house when Fearchair entered, swearing fearfully. "Is 'Nossing' in?" he enquired angrily of the boy's father. "Why are you asking for him?" demanded the other. "To shoot him as dead as a crow," roared Fearchair furiously, "for he is truly a son of the devil. He stole my shot, and spoiled my night's sport. I wish that he and J— K— and M'K— of F— were burning in the flames of hell. I could willingly sit beside them to see them properly punished." It would appear that J— K— and M'K— of

F— were as bad as " Nossing " for teasing the Wanderer. Fearchair's plan for smoking the rooks was to place a quantity of sulphur at the bottom of the trees on which they were perched, and to set fire to a long paper match, the end of which was to be placed in the sulphur, when, by inhaling the fumes, the rooks would become giddy and fall down, and then become an easy prey.

CHAPTER IV.—Self-Esteem.

No Beggar—Or Pauper—New Shirts—Fine Sport—English
Sermons—Burnt Bannocks—The Inquisitive Pig—Shaving—
The Laird's Fool—The Poor's Money—The Tender Passion—
Chief of the Clan.

It has already been indicated that Fearchair-
a-Ghunna entertained no mean opinion of himself, and numerous stories are told of the naive
manner in which he sometimes made this
known. He called one day at the kitchen door
of a certain farmer's house in the parish of
Redcastle, and, the girl in charge having offered
him the usual allowance of cake given to members of the wandering class, he indignantly
refused it, saying, "*Cha ghabh mi e bho'n a
tha thu gabhail suim dhiom mar anrach bochd*,"
i.e., "I will not take it because you're treating
me as if I were a beggar." "No, no," said the
girl, "I don't put you on a level with that
class of people. On the contrary, I consider
you a real gentleman." "*Tha thu na do
dheagh chaileag*," *i.e.*, "You are a good girl,"
said Fearchair, as he patted her on the
shoulder, "*Gabhaidh mi am bonnaich*," *i.e.*,
"Give me the cake." He got it and ate it
heartily.

A farmer from the parish of Petty who was
going to Fairburn, met with a woman belonging

to the parish of Redcastle, and as she was going the same road with himself for some distance, they walked together. When near Redcastle they came upon Fearchair, who was sitting at the road-side with his load of iron and bones on his back. The woman, after talking with him for a short time, at length suggested he should apply for Parochial relief. He at once got into a passion, indignantly repudiating any such idea, and declaring that he was far above taking anything of the kind. The woman, being acquainted with him, then offered him a few coppers, and the Petty farmer offered him a sixpenny piece, but he would take neither, saying that he was no beggar, but a strong and independent man, who required assistance from no one, adding "*An do thairgeadh dhomhsa an t-airgiod air son fudar 's luaithe a cheannach ghabhainn e*," *i.e.*, "Had you offered me the money to buy powder or shot I would have taken it."

A Ferintosh lady, who had taken some considerable interest in Fearchair's bodily comfort, gave a small sum of money one day to a dressmaker, Mrs. Mackenzie, who then resided, and still resides, at Tore Gate, to purchase cotton and make a couple of shirts for him. On finishing the shirts, Mrs. Mackenzie sent a message to Fearchair that she wished to see him. He went, and being told why he was sent for, he immediately asked how she had got the shirts—whether she got them from the

(Parochial) Board. He said—"*Ma fhuair thu iad bho'n a Bhord faodaidh thu iad a chumail d'uit fein cha bhi gnothach agamsa riutha*," or, "If you got them from the Board you may keep them yourself, as I will have nothing to do with them." Mrs. Mackenzie assured him that the Board knew nothing about them, but apparently wishing to take advantage of the dressmaker, Fearchair then declared that he would only take the shirts on condition that she would wash them for him when dirty. This the woman consented to do, and he took them.

He called at the same lady's house at Tore Gate on a New Year's day, and the door happening to be shut at the time, he began to knock at it somewhat lustily, but as the inmates were busy at the time, the door was not opened so readily as Fearchair expected. This greatly disconcerted him, and he knocked at the door with greater force than before, saying—"*O nach fosgail sibh an doruis dhomh mo chairdean ionmhuinn air fhaicum duibh gu' d'rinn mi sealg cho math*," *i.e.*, "Oh! wont you open the door to me, my dear friends, seeing that I have succeeded in making such a fine shooting." He had a dead crow in his hand, which he had picked up by the way, and hence his exclamation regarding his sport.

He frequently attended the English services in the Church of Redcastle, while the late Rev. John Kennedy lived, and, being asked why he

did so, seeing that he could not understand a
word of English, he answered proudly—"*Tha
mi feuchainn a bhi mar mo choimeas inbhe,
daoin-uaiseala na duthaich. Cha' n'eil mor-chuis
ann a bhi dol a chluinntinn searmon Gaidhlig
tha air eisdeach le sluagh cumanta a mhain*,"
i.e., "I am trying to be like my equals, the
rest of the gentlemen in the country.   There is
no pride in going to hear a Gaelic sermon,
to which only common people listen."

He was going on another Sabbath day to
hear a sermon on the occasion of a Sacramental
Communion at Redcastle, and having been
overtaken on the road by a person who was
also going thither, the latter addressing him,
said—"You are going to church to hear a
sermon to-day, Fearchair."   "*Chan eil*," he
replied, "*ach tha mi a dol do'n a bhocsa airson
an aobhar sin*," *i.e.*, "No, I am not, but I am
going to the box for that purpose." Fearchair,
as already mentioned, could understand Gaelic
only, and on such occasions as that referred to,
Gaelic congregations in the north always wor-
ship in the open air, a wooden tent being
provided for the clergyman, out of which he
addresses the people, hence Fearchair's allusion
to the " box " in his answer.

The Ross-shire Wanderer called one day at
a certain farmer's house in the parish of Redcastle, and the servant in charge gave him a
basin of broth, but she unwittingly gave him a
spoon with a broken handle and a piece of

cake which was overdone in the cooking. Fearchair looked at the spoon and bread for a second or so, and then said—" *Se spainn briste agus bonnach loisgte nithean de bheag shuim agus nithean nach bu choir a bhi air a thairgseadh gu brath do dhuin' uasal,*" *i.e.,* "A broken spoon and a burnt bannock are things of little value, and things which should never be offered to a gentleman," and, entering apparently into the spirit of prophecy, he addressed the girl thus—" *Ach bho'n a thug thu na nithean sin dhomhsa is spainn briste agus bonnach loisgte a bhitheas ann ad' chompanaich ri do bheo,*" *i.e.,* "But as you have given such things to me, a broken spoon and a burnt bannock will be your partners through life."

With such opinions of his own status it was only what might be expected if he was bitter in resenting an insult, and the incidents recorded of his early life show that he was naturally prone to take revenge. The following incidents show that he was both sensitive and vindictive.

Being on one of his customary tours in the parish of Kirkhill, he got a night's lodging in a cottar's house at Inchberry, a bed of straw being prepared for him on the floor in a corner of the kitchen. The sole occupant of the cottage was an old woman, who kept a pig, and this animal was quietly sleeping in a wisp of straw close to Fearchair's "shake-down." Towards morning the pig became restive, and at length, finding it had a neighbour, it began to take observations, which were anything but agreeable to Fearchair, especially when it commenced to poke his nose with its snout. " *Cha 'n eil e na chleachdadh aig aon a bhi gam' phogadh agus cha leig mise leat sin a dheanamh an dara uair*," said he, addressing the pig, *i.e.*, " No one is in the habit of kissing me, and I will not allow you to do it a second time." He immediately rose, seized porky by the hind legs, and knocked out its brains against the wall of the house, and at once left the place, exclaiming—" *A bhean! a bhean! tha do mhuc dhubh fo 'n chuthach*," *i.e.*, " Wife! wife! your black pig is in a fearful fit of rage." He told afterwards that he killed the pig because the old woman put him to sleep with it, remarking " *Cuiridh mise 'n geall nach dean i a rithisd e*," *i.e.*, " I'll bet a penny she'll not do it again."

He was, on another occasion, passing a camp of tinkers on the heights of Kilcoy. The tinkers began to make fun of poor Fearchair, and asked him, among other things, why he was not shaving. He answered that he was better at shaving others than himself, and that it was with his knife (which he took out of his pocket and exhibited) that he usually shaved, adding that he would gladly show his skill on any of them. The tinkers wisely declined his services as a barber, but in order to make further sport of him, they told him to shave their horse which was grazing close by, and which was more

needful than any of themselves. Fearchair
agreed, and began operations, but immediately
cut the animal's throat. "*Tachraidh tubaistean
doibhsan is ealanta,*" *i.e.,* "Accidents happen
to the most skilful," said Fearchair, smiling in
a manner altogether peculiar to himself, when
he saw the blood gushing out of the wound,
but as soon as the animal fell he ran off,
shouting "*Tha sin taghta. Nuair a mhagas tu
a rithisd, fiach do ealantachd air amadan na's
motha na Fearchair,*" *i.e.,* "That's capital.
When you mock again, try your skill on a
greater fool than Fearchair." It is fully believed that he would have treated the tinker
who spoke in the same manner as he did the
horse, had he trusted himself in his hands.

There was a time when every family of rank
in the Highlands had its fool — generally a
feigned one, and the Highland laird's fool
was usually considered the wisest man on his
estate. He therefore always sat next to his
lord on the *dais*, and dressed second to none
in the family. The fame of Fearchair's wit
soon spread far and wide, and as a consequence,
rich and poor, young and old, eagerly sought
his society, of which no one, until he lapsed
into old age, ever tired. A certain laird, re-
siding on the western confines of the Black
Isle, took a particular liking to him, and
resolved to make him his fool. So the next
time Fearchair called at the "big house" he
was most sumptuously entertained, after which

he gave ample proof of his wit. The laird was so pleased that he caused Fearchair to be forthwith attired in an excellent suit of clothes, and then told him that he was to remain with him, and share the comforts of the " big house " henceforth, while he lived. " *Cha'n fhuirich mi ann an taigh duine sam bith na's fhaide na's toil leam*," *i.e.*, " I will stay in no man's house longer than I choose," said Fearchair, as he unceremoniously threw off the suit of fine clothes, and donned his old ragged garments. " *Cha'n fhuirich mi le duine sam bith, oir tha mi na 'm shealgair mur 's aithne dhuibh agus suibhlaidh mi troimh an duthaich le mo ghunna, mar dhuin uasal eile*," *i.e.*, " I will stay with no man, for I am a hunter, as you know, and I will travel through the country with my gun, like all other gentlemen." Fearchair at once left the " big house," and it is said that he never again visited it. Although the laird was greatly disappointed by Fearchair's contemptuous refusal of his proffered kindness, he, nevertheless, showed a hearty interest in him every time he met him on the public road thereafter.

Fearchair's repugnance to become a recipient of Parochial relief is, perhaps, more clearly demonstrated by the following incident than any other. A certain Black Isle gentleman, who is still living, met Fearchair one day, and made him a present of a pound note. This circumstance having come to the knowledge of his neighbours, some of them determined to tease him, so they said—" You have taken the poor's money at last, Fearchair, it was it that Mr G— gave you." This he stoutly denied, declaring it was a present; but on their insisting that it was the poor's money, he directly proceeded to his donor's residence, and proffered him the pound note, saying— " *A bheil thu smuaineachadh gu'm biodh e ceart dhiomsa, tha comasach cothrom ceud de dh' iarruinn a ghiulan bho'n a Chanonaich, gu Inbhiruis, timchioll a Mhanachainn deirce na sgireachd a ghabhail? Cha dean mi leithid a ni,*" i.e., "Do you think, sir, it would be right of me, who am able to carry a hundred-weight of iron from Fortrose, by Beauly, to Inverness, to take Parochial relief? I will do no such thing." The gentleman assured Fearchair that he had given him the pound note as a present, and that it had nothing to do with Parochial matters. He was at length persuaded to retain the pound, and pay no heed to what silly people might say. Fearchair returned to Tarradale with the note, and a light heart to the bargain. He frequently afterwards said that Mr G— was the best and greatest gentleman in the country.

Fearchair-a-Ghunna was at one time under the sway of the tender passion. A certain young lady, of a prepossessing appearance, lived in the western district of the Black Isle, for whom our hero expressed a particular

fondness. This fact coming to the knowledge
of some light-headed youths in his neighbourhood, they began to chaff and tease him about
her, and even questioned his ability to address
her properly. They would remark — " You
will not know when you call upon her what
to say to her, Fearchair," to which they were
answered snappishly—" *Cha do chual mi riamh
mu neach sam bith chaidh cearr air a chuis sin.
'Do chual thusa ?* " *i.e.*, " I never heard of any
one who went wrong on that score. Did
you ?" Being pressed to tell what he would
say if he went to "pop" the question, he said
—" *Dhinnsinn 'dhi da ni mo chrannchar—
gu'm bheil mi na mo dhuin' uasal—sealgair da
righribh, gu'm bheil mi ann an gaol leatha—
agus gh' abairinn aig an am cheudna 'am pos thu
mi mo chaileag bhoidheach, agus bi n'ad' bhean
do shealgair ?* " *i.e.*, " I would just tell her my
position in life—that I am a gentleman—a
real hunter—that I am in love with her, and
then say — ' Will you marry me, my bonny
lass, and be a hunter's wife ? ' "

It is well known that every Highland sept
or clan had a Chief in olden times. Who
occupied that important position in the Clan
MacLennan we are not able to say ; but Fearchair-a-Ghunna frequently declared that he
himself was the " Chief of the Clan Maclennan,"
and when he thus considered himself the
principal individual of his race, we need not
wonder that he should spurn Parochial relief.

CHAPTER V.—Ingenuity.

A Merry-go-round—Fortifying the Garrison—An Enemy's
Cornfield—Sanctifying the Sabbath—A Blaster's Device—
An Iron Comforter—Hoarding—Pilfering.

Like many ill-balanced minds, Fearchair's
was capable of much subtlety, and sometimes
showed extraordinary inventive power. A
Ferintosh farmer took him at one time into his
service as herd, a duty which he satisfactorily
performed till the Sunday of the Sacramental
Communion in the "Burn." He wished much
to be with the thousands who worshipped God
there that day, but as there was no kind of
enclosure for the horses and cattle he could not
possibly leave them, and, therefore, set his
wits going, and soon hit upon the following
plan. He tied horses and cattle head to tail,
no easy task, so that they formed a large circle.
He then set off to the "Burn," while his
charge kept going round and round in the
same path till observed by some parties going
home from the preaching in the evening, when
the poor beasts were released.

Fearchair was frequently annoyed in the
"Garrison" by a lot of neighbouring boys, who
delighted in teasing him. One day a man who

happened to pass near the "Garrison," was astonished to see Fearchair on his knees near the door, evidently busy doing something. In order to satisfy his curiosity, the man approached him, and found that he was carefully sticking pins, points upward, in the ground, in a zigzag line. On his asking Fearchair what he meant by so novel a proceeding, he was answered :—"*Tha mi na-huile h-oidhche air mo phianadh le graisg de balaichean ladurna agus tha mi cur na prinneachain so anns an talamh, a chum nuair a thig na balaich a rithisd, gu'm bi iad air am peanasachadh, oir gun teagamh, lotaidh na dealgan na casan aca,*" or, "I am every night tormented by a lot of impudent, bare-footed boys, and I am placing these pins in the ground in order that when the boys come again they may be punished, for the pins will, without fail, pierce their feet." Fearchair, however, had other and more important motives for sticking the pins in the ground than for punishing the boys. A half-witted fellow called Donald Coll, who hailed from the neighbourhood of Conon bridge, used to go every Saturday evening to Fearchair's house to make sport of him. Coll was as fleet as a hind, so that Fearchair could not catch him, though he often tried to do so. He also was bare-footed, and it was more especially to punish him that Fearchair put the pins in the ground.

The next Saturday evening after the pins

had been put in position, Fearchair, placing himself behind his door, patiently waited for Coll's arrival. Immediately he came near to the " Garrison," he was pricked by the pins, and roared in agony. As soon as Coll was pierced, Fearchair, who was armed with a sickle, rushed out to him with the full intention of cutting off one of his arms, which he positively would have done but for the timely arrival of a neighbour, who prevented him from carrying his purpose into practice, which interference annoyed Fearchair a good deal.

Although there was no great danger of any person entering Fearchair's " Garrison " in his absence, and although there was neither lock nor bar on its door, it was, nevertheless, well provided against any sudden or unexpected visit. Fearchair had the blade of a scythe fixed in such a manner above the door that when opened by any person but himself, the blade would come down in guillotine style and do mortal injury. Few people, however, ever darkened his door at any time, and these did so out of curiosity. No one ever entered the house in his absence, but on one occasion a neighbour collected some cart loads of bones and other filthy matter which were lying about the house causing a disagreeable smell, and emptied them into a pit in the neighbouring wood. On discovering this, Fearchair became furious, declaring that he would be revenged on the man for interfering with his goods. He went to the man's cornfields, and wreaked his vengeance on him by sticking a number of iron spikes and pieces of wire among the corn, which had a desired effect, for when the man began to shear his corn, his scythes were quite destroyed.

Fearchair frequently went on Sundays to a certain gentleman's residence to get his dinner, but before giving it to him, the servants were in the habit of making him go for the coals to the cellar. Having no great liking for work at any time, and the coal cellar being difficult of access, this Sunday employment was anything but congenial to his mind, and he soon contrived a plan for escaping it. On Saturday evening he went to the house in question, and told the servants that he had come to inform them that the following day was Sabbath. "*Bi deas air a shon*," he continued, "*oir cha'n fhaod obair a bhi air a dheaneamh air an la sin feumaidh an guail a tha air a chomharrachadh airson ant sabaid a bhi anns an aite shuidhichte air Di-sathiurne*," or, "Be prepared for it, as no work must be done on that day—have all the coals you may require for Sabbath in their proper place on Saturday." "He did not give these instructions," says our informant, "for any special regard he had for the Sabbath, but in order to avoid the carrying of the coals, which he was compelled to do ere he got his dinner." His device was crowned with success.

Fearchair continued to take an interest in
blasting stones till within a short period of his
death. A few months prior to that event, he
was blasting a stone for a neighbour at Tarradale. The stone being very hard, Fearchair
took a longer time to bore it than he anticipated,
and ere he was ready to put in the charge the
night grew dark, and the operation was post-
poned till next day. On preparing to go
home, some of the youths who were looking on
said to him that they would put the charge in
and fire it. " *Cha dean sibh sin*," *i.e.*, " You
wont do that," said Fearchair, as he proceeded
to fill up the hole with clay, which he pressed
so hard that it took him a considerable time
next day to clear it out.

We may mention here that Fearchair had
an apprehension that his death would come by
the hand of an assassin, who would strangle
him, and to provide against this he had several
pieces of chain rolled round his neck. These
chains, which were constantly worn, were as
bright and glittering as silver, and were as
much prized by him as if they had been made
of gold.

As he never spent any of the pennies and
sixpences he received from the charitable public,
nor of the proceeds of his peculiar wares (except
the little he paid for powder and shot), he was
able to save a considerable sum of money from
time to time; but no person had the remotest
idea of the place where he kept it—that Fear-

chair kept a profound secret. When asked by a certain party where he stored his pelf, he answered wittily, "*Tha e air adhlachdadh agam ann an toll 's an talamh, agus 'nuair tha mi air mo shineadh 's-an uaigh laidhidh m'airgiod far am bheil e, falaichte agus dichui-mhnte, i.e.,* "I have it buried in a hole in the earth; and when I am laid in my grave my money will lie where it is, concealed and forgotten." As he predicted, the money, so far as known to us, has not been discovered to the present day. He hid a good many other curiosities in the same way.

Fearchair-a-Ghunna was of considerable service to his neighbours at Tarradale, for he would thrash any amount of corn for them for a mere nominal remuneration. He was at one time thrashing some oats for his next door neighbour, and the landlady noted that after his coming to the barn she failed to find a single hen's egg. Although she did not suspect Fearchair of having anything to do with the disappearance of the eggs, she nevertheless determined to watch his movements on a certain day. Fearchair's work that day was smashing bones in the barn close to where the hens roosted. The landlady had not been long watching his proceedings when she saw him go to the hen's nest, and she at once shouted, "What are you doing there, Fearchair?" He immediately answered, "*Tha thu na do bhoir-rionnach ro gheur. 'Se cnaimh a th'am*

D

*a leum bho'n urlar gus a'nead agus tha mi
direach ga toir a mach,*" *i.e.*, "You are a
very sharp woman. It is only a bone that
sprang from the floor to the nest, and I am
just trying to get it out." But having had her
suspicions thus aroused, and not being so easily
deceived as Fearchair imagined, she resolved
to keep a sharp watch upon him while he
remained at her premises. The result was
that when he was leaving for home she noticed
that he went to a thicket of broom which grew
in rear of the house, and carried something away.
She at once ran after him, and found that he
was carrying a pot which was three-fourths full
of eggs. This circumstance shows that Fearchair was not strictly honest in his latter days,
and also shows that he was in no way influenced
by that piety which his answers to the clergy
and his ejaculatory prayers indicated. The
above is the only instance of his dishonesty
that we have heard of, and but for our having
received the information from a son of the
woman referred to, we would have been reluc-
tant to put it on record.

Fearchair, who was often out for a whole
night in search of game in his own peculiar
way, came one cold, drizzly morning to a
certain cottage which stood at the foot of the
hill whereon he had been engaged in a fruitless
hunt all night. The sole occupant of the
cottage was a maiden lady, and Fearchair
conceived the idea that if he could get into

the woman's warm bed (she had not then risen), he would get the warmth and sleep of which he stood in need. For this purpose he forced his way into the cottage, and without any further ado, threw off his wet garments and jumped under the blankets beside the astonished woman, who, with one bound, sprang to the middle of the floor, pouring a volley of her choicest Billingsgate on the Wanderer's head for his unseemly conduct. He thanked her kindly for leaving the bed to himself, and then told her that as he was bent on having a snooze she might dry his clothes at the fire.

CHAPTER VI.—Quaint Remarks.

Satan's Hair — A Big Fool — Where God is not—Religious
Topics—The Miller's Swine—The Belle's Likeness—Education
—A Scanty Allowance—The Hearse—Hornless Sheep—Wasps
and Good Boys—The Parish Minister—The Cat's Sabbath—
The Devil's Funeral.

Fearchair - a - Ghunna had not been long
settled in the Black Isle when the fame of
his wit and sarcastic answers had spread far
and wide, and often formed the topic of conversation at many a gathering during the
long winter nights. Hundreds of people who
had never seen him enthusiastically applauded
his sayings, and many bets regarding his
merits and demerits were won and lost at
these gatherings. An arrogant young man in
the west end of the Black Isle, who ridiculed
Fearchair's wit, as well as the sagacity of
those who came in contact with him, one
night wagered ten to one that he would give
the Wanderer a question which he could not
answer. The bet was taken, and Fearchair
was asked to go next evening to a certain
house close at hand. Fearchair went, and a
large number of people assembled to hear the
question and the answer. Immediately on

Fearchair being seated, the hero of acuteness asked him, " What is the colour of Satan's hair ? " Without a moment's hesitation Fearchair said, " *Am bheil thu cho fada ann an seirbheis Shatan agus nach eil eolais agad air dath fhuilt do mhaighstir ?* " *i.e.*, " Are you so long in the devil's service and don't know the colour of your master's hair yet ? " He then looked round the company and burst into a hearty laugh, in which he was joined by all present, his questioner included.

A certain lady meeting Fearchair one day, asked him how it happened that he was such a big fool ? to which he readily answered, " *O, 'se coire m' athar 'tha ann. Bha fhios aig gun robh mi deitheil air a ghunna agus sitheann, agus 'gam a theagasg na rocais a mharbhadh rinn e amadain dhiom, ach cha d' rinn aon dhiom cho mhor's tha thusa,*" *i.e.*, " Oh ! it is my father's fault ; he knew I was fond of the gun and venison, and in teaching me to shoot rooks, made a fool of me, but not such a big one as you are." The lady resolved never to ask such a question again.

On another occasion a young man meeting Fearchair addressed him thus :—" Of all the fools I ever saw, I think you are the greatest." The Wanderer replied, " *Tha mi creidsinn gum bheil thugad, smuaineachadh fhein na do dhuine gle ghlic, ach le do ghliocas agus innleachd, agus mo choltas amaideachd, fiach an toir thu an car asam-sa, agus ma shoirbhicheas*

leat bheir mise crun duit," or, "I believe you
think yourself a very wise man; but with all
your wisdom and ingenuity, and my apparent
silliness, try if you can cheat me, and if you
succeed I will give you a crown." The man
admitted that Fearchair was right—that he
could not be cheated. This man and the
subject of our sketch were familiarly acquainted
from boyhood.

Being on one of his customary rounds, one
day he was met on the public road by a certain
Ross-shire clergyman, who, having heard about
the Wanderer's wit, asked him if he knew
where God was? Fearchair at once answered
—"*O! nach thu an t-amadan—nach inns
thu dhomhsa c'aite nach eil e?*" *i.e.,* "Oh!
what a fool you are—can you tell me where
He is not?" "You are quite right, Fearchair," observed the minister, "God is every-
where, and we should always remember that
His all-seeing eyes are upon us." "*Cha'n eil
mi smuaineachadh gu'm bheil Dia anns na
h-uile h-aite,*" *i.e.,* "I don't think God is in
every place," said Fearchair, as he moved away.

Among others who heard of the manner in
which Fearchair silenced the minister was the
miller of Redcastle, a shrewd, intelligent man.
To puzzle Fearchair the next time he came
round, the miller determined to ask him the
question which he himself had put to the clergyman. When Fearchair called at the miller's
house, therefore, and as soon as circumstances

would permit, Fearchair was asked if he could tell him of any place where God was not? to which he (Fearchair) immediately replied— "*Cha'n eil Dia ann an cridhe an duine neo-iompaichte*," or, "God is not in the heart of an unconverted man." "Well, well," said the miller, "what a wonder, Fearchair, that the minister did not think of that."

Some strange ineptitude seemed to be connected with the manner in which the clergyman interrogated Fearchair. He called one day at the manse of a well-known Ross-shire minister, and after being hospitably entertained, the minister asked him if he was afraid of death? "*Cha'n eil gu dearbh. Cha'n eil*," or, "No, indeed, I am not," was Fearchair's reply. "Does anything at all frighten you?" asked the other in astonishment. "*O! tha. Tha eagal orm roimh sin a tha air an taobh eile do 'n bhas*," or, "Oh! yes. I am afraid of that which is beyond death," answered Fearchair, assuming his interrogator's Sunday gravity.

Having called at the same manse on another occasion, the clergyman, no doubt struck with Fearchair's former laconic answer, was determined to give him a puzzler for once, at anyrate. He therefore asked him if he could tell how many miracles Christ performed while He was on earth. "*Ubh! ubh!*" said Fearchair in amazement. "*Ciod a rinn E ach miorbhuilean fhad's a bha E air an talamh?*" or "What did He do but miracles while He was on earth?"

A horse died at one time near a road some
little distance south-east of Inverness, and, as
was the practice in rural districts in those days,
the carcase was allowed to lie where the animal
expired, until the dogs devoured all the flesh.
Hearing that the bones were bare and clean,
Fearchair appeared on the scene, and, gathering
the whole of them together, he carried them
on his back to Inverness. On his way thither,
he was met by a farmer from the estate of
Inches, who said—" You have a nasty and
heavy burden on your back, Fearchair." The
latter replied—" *Tha eallach ni's graineil agus
ni's motha na bheil thusa faicinn orm, mo dhuine
mhath,*" or "I have a more ugly and greater
burden than what you see, my good man."
"What is that?" asked the farmer. " *Is e
eallach uamhasaich a' pheacaidh tha mi giulan
an comhnuidh,*" *i.e.,* " It is the fearful burden of
sin which I constantly carry," said Fearchair,
and passed on with his load of bones, which he
sold in Inverness, as usual, at a fair price.

Fearchair having called at a certain miller's
house in the Black Isle on one occasion, the
miller enquired if he could mention any particular thing he knew. Upon Fearchair replying
in the affirmative, the miller asked him what it
was. He answered sharply—" *Tha fios agam
gu'm bheil na mucan agad ann an deagh
shuidheachadh,*" or, " I know that your swine
are in excellent condition." Reversing the
question, the miller asked him—" Can you tell

me something that you don't know?" to which
Fearchair replied, "*Pu! dhuine tha sin na cuis
fueasda. Cha'n eil fhios agam co leis an
an arbhair tha gum beathachadh*," or, "Pugh!
man, that is an easy matter. I don't know
whose corn feeds your swine." This was a
retort which the honest miller neither expected
nor deserved, for, although it might truly apply
to some other millers it did not to the miller in
question.

On another occasion Fearchair, who had
called at a certain house in the same parish at
the dinner hour, happened to be at the time very
hungry, and one of the landlord's daughters, a
haughty, conceited, young woman, chanced to
be in the kitchen when Fearchair entered it.
After making ridicule of him a little while, she
offered him a herring. Looking intently at her
for a moment, the Wanderer said—"Keep it
carefully as a memento of yourself, young
woman; for, every time you look at its scales
you will see a perfect likeness of your own
beauty, of which you think so much, but of
which other people think so little."

An eminent Ross-shire clergyman, famed for
his humorous wit and inexhaustible store of
anecdote, was on one occasion taking an evening walk on the public road some short distance
from his manse, when he came upon a horse
shoe lying on the road. Happening at that
moment to see Fearchair coming towards him,
and knowing that he had a peculiar liking for

old iron, the minister lifted the shoe and carried
it in his hand till he met Fearchair, when he
handed it to him saying—" Here is a horse shoe
for you, Fearchair, which I found on the road a
little way back." On receiving the shoe, Fearchair looked intently at it for some moments
and then said—" *Nach anabarrach briagh an
ni foghlum ? Bheir e eolais do dhuine thar
tomhais. Cha b'urrainn mise eadar-dheal-
achaidh a chuir oirre bho cruidhe lair,*" or,
" What a grand thing education is ! The knowledge it gives a man is really wonderful. I
would not know this from a mare's shoe." The
clergyman smiled and said, " O Fearchair,
Fearchair," and then passed on.

An anecdote somewhat similar to the pre-
ceding one appears in " Jamie Fleeman."

There was nothing Fearchair disliked more
than to receive a scanty allowance of provision
when he called at a house. He called one day
at a house in Tarradale in the landlady's absence,
and, being pretty hungry at the time, he asked
a blooming young girl who chanced to be in
the house to give him something to eat. Flora
cheerfully gave him as much cake as she thought
was sufficient to satisfy him for the time being,
but Fearchair thought otherwise, for immediately he got it he said, " I am afraid, my young
girl, that you have committed two irreparable
wrongs by giving me so much bread. In the
first place, you have injured yourself by the
weight of it, and in the second place, you have

ruined this family by giving so much of their effects away."

Jogging along the public road one day, Fearchair saw a hearse approaching him, the first one he had ever seen. He asked a man who had just come up to him what it was, and having been told, wetted one of his eyes with a spittle, and as the hearse came up to him he called out with a lamentable cry, " *Oh! beannaich mise! Ged e so, tha mi faicinn? Sginnteach gur e aon deth carbad—an dubh ifrinn a tha 'nn,*" or, " Oh! dear me, what is this I see ? surely it is one of the black coaches of hell." " The tears are only coming from one of your eyes, Fearchair," said one of the men who was along with the hearse. " Och, och," was Fearchair's ready reply, " the other eye is so stubborn that it will not shed a single tear."

When walking on one of the public roads in the Black Isle one day, Fearchair met a large drove of sheep. When the rear of the drove had passed him, a farmer appeared on the scene, and addressing a man in charge of the sheep, said—" What a beautiful flock of wedders you have got. " *Bi iad de bheag feum do nas ceaird,*" or, " They will be of little use to the tinkers," shouted Fearchair, who heard the remark, the point of the observation being that the sheep were hornless.

Resting at the roadside one day, Fearchair began to sort his bundle, as was his wont. He

was thus engaged when a wag noticed him,
and played him a trick. Fearchair was sitting
at the side of a bush, and the wag tied him to
it, and then stepped aside to see the result.
When Fearchair was sufficiently rested, he
prepared to go, but was, of course, unable to
move from the place where he was sitting.
Every time he attempted to rise he failed, and
muttered to himself, " *Nach mi tha fas lag !* "
or, " How weak I am getting ! " On finding
out the trick, however, he vowed vengeance on
its perpetrator sooner or later.

He was one day, towards the end of summer,
passing the parish school of Urray. That
summer having been unusually dry, there was
a large number of wasp " pots " throughout the
country, and at the roadside near the school
referred to there was a " pot " of great size.
On seeing Fearchair passing, it occurred to
some of the biggest schoolboys to play him
a trick, and induced him, under some pretext,
to sit down close to the wasps' pot. As soon
as he had done so, the boys struck the pot
with their sticks, and hundreds of wasps were
instantly flying about Fearchair's face, but
strange to say, none of them stung him. He sat
quite composed, looking at the boys, who were
standing at a considerable distance off, laughing
at, as they supposed, his great dilemma. Wishing, no doubt, to be revenged upon them for
the trick, he endeavoured to coax them to come
and sit beside him, by offering a penny to each

of them, an offer which they wisely declined. Seeing this he said:—" *Cha dean na speachan cron oirbh, oir tha sibh na 'r balachain maith—'se cloinn an diabhol a mhain a e loiteadh iad*," or, " The wasps will not injure you, for you are good boys—they will only hurt the devil's children." Hearing this, and being ashamed of what they had done, the boys immediately skulked away. This anecdote is told by one of the boys in question—now a grey-haired man, and in a good position in life.

Fearchair bore a special hatred to wasps, which was evinced by the determined way he set about destroying them when he chanced to find a " pot " by the wayside. It was no unusual thing to see him spending a long summer's day in his efforts to kill those little, and (when interfered with) vicious insects—a work in which he took immense delight, and which was carried on thus:—As soon as he found a wasp's " pot," he would set his gun in position—an operation which generally occupied from forty minutes to an hour—the muzzle being placed almost close to the centre of the " pot." This done, the explosion was effected in the customary way—by applying the peat, or match, to the priming—but, although the most of the " pot " and the wasps it contained at the time of the explosion, would be burned, or driven to atoms, yet hundreds of those industrious creatures would at that time be absent on the duties of their domicile, and returning in dozens every minute, a large number would be buzzing at the site of the "pot," ere Fearchair could congratulate himself on its destruction. As it would be use-less to attack them with his gun now, and being determined to annihilate them, he would set to, and continue killing them, one by one, with a broom branch, until the whole were destroyed. It was somewhat remarkable that, although mad with rage for being molested, the wasps were never known to sting him—"*Bha sìan air*," or, "He was enchanted."

A certain Ross-shire minister intimated in his church one Sabbath that he would be preaching in a particular part of his parish on a certain day. Between the time that he intimated this, however, and the day appointed, he received an urgent call to go elsewhere, to which he consented, and, of course, made this last arrangement as public as possible. There were some, however, who did not get notice, and Fearchair was among them. He went to the place and remained strolling about the "tent" all day. Shortly afterwards the minister met him, and asked him why he seemed so dull and displeased. "*Cha'n iongantach gu'm bithinn dubhach air faicinn domh gu'm bheil an donnas toir air ministeir na sgireachd a bhi'g innseadh nam breug*," or, "No wonder although I should be sad, seeing that the devil makes our parish minister tell lies," said Fearchair.

Passing through the Kilcoy district one day, Fearchair called at a house, and so soon as he

entered it he placed a dead crow, which he had
picked up by the way, on the red-hot coals.
Whenever the flesh began to broil, the flavour
spread through the house, and soon reached
the nose of the cat, to whom it was apparently
very agreeable, for it commenced to mew
lustily, hearing which, Fearchair exclaimed
angrily, " *Cum do theanga, a mheirleach !
Cha 'n fhaod tu cuid de m' fheolsa iarraidh,
oir faodaidh tu pailteas de radain agus luchan
a mharbhadh air Di-domhnaich, ni nach urrainn
mise 'dheanamh,*" or, " Hold your tongue, you
thief ! You need not ask for any of my flesh,
for you can kill plenty of rats and mice on
Sabbath, which I cannot do."

The day the first train that ran on the Ross-
shire line passed the village of Tarradale the
Wanderer happened to be there, and on seeing
it coming along at full speed from the south, he
cried, " *Sin agad a tighinn an diabhol agus
ainglean—teachdairean am bhais,*" or, " There
comes the devil with his angels—the black
messengers of death." That the train has been
the " black messenger of death " to hundreds
of the human race cannot be denied. He was
standing on the bridge that spans the railway
at Tarradale on another occasion, and as the
train came rushing along from the north he
compared it to " Old Nick's funeral."

Fearchair said one day to the ferrymen at
Kessock, who were teasing him without any
mercy, " *Tha mi gabhail iongantais nach fag*

sibh mi na m'aonar, air faicinn gu'm bheil Dia E-fhein cur suas leam cho fada," i.e., " I wonder much that you will not leave me alone, seeing God Himself is putting up with me so long."

Fearchair got a quantity of powder from some of the men working in the quarry of Tarradale, who told him to tell no one where he got it. Shortly afterwards he called at the house of a neighbour who knew of his getting the powder from the quarrymen, and to test his powers of secrecy he asked Fearchair where he got the powder. After receiving various evasive answers, the neighbour at length said, " Was it not from the men in the quarry you got it, Fearchair? " " *Mata, mata, fag a sin e,*" said the latter, " *agus bi deas leis,*" i.e., " Well, well, leave it there itself then, and be done with it."

CHAPTER VII.—Gravity and Death.

Religious Ideas—Sabbath Observance—Time for Church—
The Indian Princess—In a Thunderstorm—At Funerals—
Prayer—Last Sickness—Blasting again—The Master Passion—
The Infirmary—The End.

In spite of all his foibles, Fearchair's mind
was of a strongly religious cast. His religion,
moreover, was of the sternest kind, for he was
firmly convinced that he was by nature an
heir of eternal perdition. He believed that
an offended God rules in heaven and earth,
who will certainly punish the wicked and
unbelieving, but it cannot be said that his
walk and conversation were to any great
extent influenced by this belief, and his notions
of an over-ruling Providence may be gathered
from the following anecdote. A number of
Tomich boys were one day teasing him un-
mercifully, on which Fearchair - a - Ghunna
ejaculated the following expressive prayer—
" *O Thighearna! cia de nach urrainn duitsa
a dheanamh duinn? Tha Thu comasach sinn
a sparradh troimh tholl a 'choin, agus sinn a
luidricheadh anns an t-slochd òtraich, air sgath
ar peacaidhean,*" or, " O Lord! what canst

E

Thou not do to us? Thou art able to thrust
us out through the dog-hole, and then bedaub
us in the dung-hill pit, and all for our sins."
The dog-hole, it should be explained, was a
hole left in olden times in the masonry at the
side of the door to let the dog pass out and in
at pleasure.

Fearchair always showed a peculiar regard
for the Sabbath, and latterly he showed this
feeling by lying in bed during all that day.
On being asked his reason for this conduct,
Fearchair replied, "*Cha bhrosnaich mi Dia
le 'bhi saltradh air an talamh aig air la na
Sabaid,*" or, "I will not offend God by treading
on His ground on the Sabbath day." The
real reason, however, was that on that day a
number of idlers gathered about his door to
tease him should he come out.

Fearchair was in Kilcoy district one Saturday
evening, and having called at a certain house
there, a bed was provided for him as usual in
the barn. Fearchair did not make his appearance in the kitchen at the proper time on
Sunday morning, and wondering what had
come over him, one of the members of the
family proceeded to the barn and asked him
why he did not get up? "Don't you know,
Fearchair," said the young man, "that this is
the Sabbath day, and you ought to rise at the
proper time, like other folks?" Fearchair
replied, assuming the gravity of a saint,
"*Tha fhios agam gu'r e so la an Tighearna,*

*agus nach eil fhios agad, mo dhuine og gur e
so an la thug e do dhuine 's ainmhidh airson
taimh? Tha mise a gabhail an taimh a
thug Dia dhomh,"* or, " Why, yes, I do know
that this is the Lord's day; and don't you
know, my young man, that this is the day
which God gave to man and beast for rest?
I am only taking the rest that God gave
me."

As several of the Kilcoy people were proceeding to the church of Redcastle one
fine Sabbath day, they overtook Fearchair,
who was going to the same church. As is
often the case with country people, they
were somewhat late, and one of their number
addressing Fearchair said :—" Why are you not
running, Fearchair? we are very late to-day."
Fearchair, who was walking at his usual pace,
answered with an air worthy of the rev. gentleman whom they were going to hear, " *Ma
ghlacas an Spiorad Naomh sinn, bi sinn ann
an trath math,*" or, " If the Holy Spirit over-
takes us, we shall be in good time."

Fearchair resided for about twelve months
at a place called Stronchro, in the parish of
Urray, and while there some young men in
his neighbourhood gathered together, and con-
cocted the following novel plan in order to
induce him to attend the services in the church
of that parish every Sabbath. They called
upon him one evening, and told him of the
immense riches possessed by the pretty (they

knew he was a great admirer of beauty), though dark-skinned ladies of eastern climes ; that he needed a wife at any rate, and that it would be as well for him to marry a wealthy lady as a woman without means; that if he should marry an Indian princess, she not only would clothe him in gorgeous apparel, but she would also deck him with many chains of gold, and supply him with a silver gun; and that if he would consent to attend divine service every Sunday regularly in the church of Urray for one year from that day, they would send for and present him with one of these rich ladies. Fearchair was so captivated with the prospect of getting so much wealth, that he readily agreed to their terms, and never failed, whatever kind of weather prevailed, to put in an appearance in the church of Urray during the stipulated time. At the year's end Fearchair demanded his rich wife, and the youths, equal to the occasion, requested him to meet them on the following evening at the Tailor's house at Aultgowrie, when he would meet his oriental millionaire. At the appointed time, Fearchair and the youths appeared at the *rendezvous.* One of them was dressed as a female, whose face was carefully blackened with soot, and this person they presented to Fearchair as his rich Indian wife. On seeing his supposed future partner through life, Fearchair scanned *her* closely without uttering a word for about the space of a minute, and then addressing the youths he said, "*Ubh! Ubh! a chairdean, nach i tha oileteil dubh? 'S ann oirre tha coltas an uilc,*" or "Oh! my friends, is she not horribly black? She seems evil itself."

Immediately after he had spoken these words, the *lady*, addressing him, said that *she* wished to seal their engagement by a mutual embracing of each other; and suiting *her* words by action, *she* approached him for that purpose. Seeing this, Fearchair exclaimed wildly, "*Mar fan thu air falbh uam cuiridh mi a mhosg riut— Air sgath Dhia na tig faisg orm—Mo chairdean, cumaidh uam i,*" which may be rendered thus — "If you don't keep off from me I will shoot you with the musket—For God's sake do not come near me—My friends, keep her from me."

The last part of his utterance was addressed to the youths, who were by this time in fits of laughter. Fearchair, as quick as possible, put his musket in position, and directly he did so, he applied the fire to the powder in the usual way. Immediately the explosion took place, Fearchair exclaimed in great glee, addressing the "lady"—"*Hala, tha mi smuaineachadh gun sasaich sin thu an aite fear posda,*" or, "*Hala,* that will, I think, satisfy you instead of a husband." The "Indian *lady*" ran away, of course, without experiencing the least harm —*she* was neither hurt nor touched by the shot; and the farce thus ended.

He was blasting stones on one occasion close to where a boy was tending some cattle. The charge was exploded in the usual way, and a large splinter of the stone fell close to where Fearchair was standing. "That piece of stone came very near you, Fearchair," said the boy. "What would you do if it had struck you?" "*Bha Dia eadar mi agus an clach*," meaning "God was between me and the stone," answered Fearchair, and then laughed.

One day, during a violent and very alarming thunderstorm, some children asked Fearchair, who was in the house along with them and seemed easy and composed, whether he was not afraid that the lightning would kill him. Assuming a most solemn appearance, he replied gravely, "*Cha'n eil d' ar-righibh, oir ma bhitheas mi air mo mharbhadh leis an dealanach, gheibh mi theagamh cuil air neamh*," i.e., "No, indeed, I am not, for if I am killed by the lightning, I shall, perhaps, get a corner in heaven."

Fearchair attended all the funerals in the district. Having gone to the funeral of a dowager-lady, who was noted for her hospitality to the poor of the parish, and who had been particularly kind to the Wanderer, he received several glasses of whisky and a supply of bread and cheese, along with the others who had gathered for the funeral. When the mournful *cortége* was about to start for the place of interment, Fearchair noticed many poor people weeping. "*Tha ioghnadh orm*," he said, "*cho*

*rag 'sa tha mo shuilean; tha iad a diultadh aon
deur a shileadh—ach ged tha mo shuilean tioram,
tha bron mo chridhe airson am beanoircheasach
a dh' fhalbh, tha mi cinnteach nach mo na 'n
duilcheadas iadsan a tha deanamh mor chuis
de'm broin,"* or "I am astonished; how stiff my
eyes are—they refuse to shed a single tear; but
although my eyes are dry, the sorrow of my
heart for my departed benefactress is, I am
sure, far greater than the sorrow of those who
make a show of their grief." No doubt, Fearchair spoke the real truth, for the sorrow of
many is superficial.

The Ross-shire Wanderer's prayer has already
been alluded to. We shall now give as complete
a version of it as we could obtain, for it is as
curious a prayer as ever was written. Every
effort has been used to procure a perfect copy
of it, as no person could correctly repeat
more than one fourth of it. It is also necessary to say that much of its pathos is lost in
the translation.

URNUIGH-NA-CREUBHAIG.

*O Thrionaid Bheannaichte tha Thu ann America
agus Australia agus tha Thu ann an so an drasda.
Tha Thu mar an iasg air an dubhan cha leig an
reothairt dheth Thu. O Thusa 'Thrionaid Bheannaichte. Tha Thu ann an so an drasda, agus anns
a' Ghaidhealtachd, agus an ann Inbhirnis 's air na
stiopallan arda. Tha Thu 'n so an drasda, agus sios*

aig Bail'a-Dhuthaich. Tha Thu toirt taighean scleata
do na h-uaislean, ach thug Thu dhomh-sa a mhain
bothan dubh suidheach nach cum a mach boinn' uisge
—na h-uile deur a tuiteam ann am brochan Fhearchair. Beannaich an gobha a dhealbhas a' chruaidh
a ghearras an t-iarunn air son a' sparradh anns na
clachan. Beannaich an talamh, O Thrionaid, agus
làthaich, a'chearc bhuidhe leis na h-eoin, am bo
(no mhart) bhàn, am bainne, agus na caoraich, dean-
O Thrionaid Bheannaichte. Beannaich mar an ceudna
na h-eich, cairtean (na cuirn) croinn, agus cliathainn,
an coirce, an t-eorna, agus am buntata, an teine, an
t-uisge, agus na h-uile seorsa de shoitheachain—seadh,
beannaich iad, O Thrionaid Bheannaichte. Beannaich na craobhan, am feur, agus moine, an connusg,
am fraoch, an rainich, agus an aitionn. Beannaich
mar an ceudna, O Thrionaid, na gunnachan, am fudar,
agus luaidhe; na rocaise, pioghaidean, cearcan-
fhraoich, cearcan-thomain, maighich agus coinneanan
—dean, O Thrionaid Bheannaichte, Beannaich mar an
ceudna na feidh, na h-earban, na lachan fiadhaich agus
callaidh, na geoidh, na faoillinéan, na coin agus na
cait na luchan, radannan agus fathan thalmhain—
dean, O Thrionaid Bheannaichte. Beannaich, mar an
ceudna, an iasg anns a mhuir (a chuan) loch, abhainn,
agus sruth, ach beannaich gu h-araidh an sgadan
mor maith a tha sinn faighinn leis a' bhuntata. Agus
beannaich, O Thrionaid Bheannaichte, na pioban
tombaca, cruaidh, agus clachan spor, cnamhan, itean,
luideagan, uichraichean agus iarrunn. Beannaich
mar an ceudna am fiodh, cainbe, cotain, agus ti 's
siucair, ged nach eil cuibhrionn Fhearchair bhochd

*dhuibh ach beag. Beannaich a h-uile ni, O Thrionaid
Bheannaichte, oir Chruthaich Thusa, Thu-fhein, iad
uile.—Amen.*

"O blessed Trinity, Thou art in America and
Australia, and Thou art here just now. Thou art like
the fish on the hook—the high-tide will not let Thee
off. O Thou art the Blessed Trinity. Thou art here
just now, and Thou art in the Highlands, and in Inverness, and on the high steeples. Thou art here just
now, and east at Tain. Thou art giving slated houses
to the big folk, but Thou hast only given a black
sooty bothy to me, which won't keep out a rain drop
—every drop falling into Fearchair's brochan (gruel).
Bless the smith who makes the steel which cuts the
iron for to be driven into the stones. Bless the earth,
O Trinity, and the gutter—the yellow hen with the
chickens; the white cow, the milk, and the sheep—
do, O blessed Trinity. Bless also the horses, carts,
ploughs, and harrows, the oats, barley, and potatoes ;
the fire, water, and all kinds of dishes—yes, bless
them, O blessed Trinity. Bless the trees, grass, and
peats ; the broom, whins, heather, brackens, and
juniper. Bless likewise, O Trinity, the guns, powder,
and shot ; the rooks, magpies, moorfowl, partridges,
hares, and rabbits—do, O blessed Trinity. Bless also
the deer, the roes, the wild ducks and tame ones ; the
geese, the gulls, the dogs, and cats, the mice, rats, and
moles—do, O blessed Trinity. Bless likewise the
fish in the sea, lake, river, and stream ; but bless, more
especially, the good big herring that we get with the
potatoes. And bless, O blessed Trinity, the pipes,

tobacco, steel, and flints; the bones, feathers, rags, keys, and iron. Bless also the wood, hemp, cotton, and tea and sugar—although poor Fearchair's share of them be small. Bless every thing, O blessed Trinity, for Thou Thyself has created all.—Amen."

Fearchair, for many years, would readily repeat this prayer for a few coppers, but he ultimately got so disgusted by people who were anxious to hear it, that, when told to say it, he would run away in great anger, exclaiming, " *B'e urnuigh mo chreich i; bu mhaith dhomh nach dubhairt mi riamh i,*" or " It is the prayer of my ruin ; it were better for me I had never said it."

Highlanders are credited, rightly or wrongly, with being good singers and fair poets, but whether Fearchair was skilled in the former we have not heard; and the following stanza, which we give in his own vernacular Gaelic, will give an idea of his knowledge of the latter :

A chreubhag mo ruin, seall a mach's thu air leth shuil,
A dh-fheuchainn am faic thu pioghaid mo ghaol,
Na'n rocas mor dubh, a dh' eigheas gun sguir,
'N uair tha'd a spuinneadh buntata 's eorn'.

TRANSLATION.

O body, my dear, look far beyond here,
And try can'st thou see, though thy eye single be—
My lovely magpie, or the rook that soars high,
And plunders potatoes and barley.

A millwright from the district of Culloden was at work on one occasion in a certain part of Redcastle. One Sabbath morning one of the young women in the house where the millwright was staying requested him to go along with her to the barn where Fearchair was sleeping, to hear his prayer. He agreed, and they both went to the barn, and after some little coaxing on the part of the young lady, Fearchair repeated his prayer — *Urnuigh-na-Creubhaig*—and the solemn manner in which he did so, strange as the prayer was, had the effect of giving him a very high place in the millwright's estimation, who took him to be a real Christian. No sooner did the young lady begin to tease Fearchair than the millwright changed his good opinion of him, " for he cursed and swore," said the millwright, " in the most awful manner it is possible to conceive. He invoked the Almighty to send fire and brimstone speedily to consume both the girl and myself. I thought every moment an hour till I got beyond his reach. I never heard anything to equal Fearchair's oaths."

When upwards of eighty years of age Fearchair-a-Ghunna was as keen a sportsman as he had ever been, though scarcely so fit for his favourite employments of shooting and blasting. In the autumn of 1868 he was one day out fishing in the neighbourhood of Fairburn, where he was met by a brother angler who had a flask of spirits. Fearchair was made welcome to the latter, but he was now becoming old and infirm, and the spirits affected his brain more readily than they would have done at an earlier period, the consequence on this occasion being that in trying to go home he lost his way. Next morning he was found lying in a wood nearly dead from the effects of the over-dose and the subsequent exposure. A kindly neighbour had him conveyed home in a cart, but, as has already been shown, there were no comforts for the sick in poor Fearchair's house. His bed consisted of formless heaps of rags, and here, with little or no attendance or assistance, Fearchair lay for several days thereafter unable to rise. The state of affairs coming to the ears of Mr. Maclennan of Hilton, that gentleman set about getting Farquhar's house cleaned and his needs properly attended to. But Fearchair's ruling passion was as strong as ever, and he forbade them, under pain of his malediction, to touch any of his possessions. A few days after this sickness had commenced, a neighbour, who went to see him, not imagining that his " sickness was unto death," spoke to Fearchair about a large stone which was in his field, and which he wished removed if possible. " *Cuiridh sinn as di,*" or " We will destroy it," said the sick man; and, although barely able to move by reason of weakness, he proceeded to the stone and commenced boring it. The neighbour accompanied him, and noticing that when he sat down he could scarcely get up again, asked him what was wrong with him? Fear-chair answered that something *was* wrong with him, but could not tell what it was. He, however, managed to blast the stone, return home to his house, and get to bed. As he continued to sink, he was removed to a neighbour's house, and about a week afterwards he was carried in a cart to the Northern Infirmary at Inverness. He strongly objected to be removed from his own house, declaring that he would return to it as soon as he would be able to do so. He never did return. While in the Infirmary he became chargeable to the parish of Contin, Ross-shire.

Fearchair had not been long in the Northern Infirmary when he perceived that his end was fast approaching, and he considered it proper to give some instructions regarding his inter-ment. Addressing his attendant one day, he said, " *Tha fhios agam nach eirich mi gu brath dheth an leabaidh so. Tha mi basachadh, agus 'nuair tha mi marbh, bu mhiann leam mo chorp a bhi air adhlacadh ann an Cill Srath-Chonain, le m'athraichean 's mo luchd daimh. Mur bi m' iarrtas air a choimhlionadh, bi mallachdan m' anma 's mo chuirp a gabhail seilbh annaibh,*" or, " I know that I shall never rise off this bed—I am dying, and when I am dead I wish my body to be buried in the Churchyard of Strathconon, along with my fathers and kindred. If my request is not attended to, the curses of my soul and body will rest on you."

Fearchair-a-Ghunna died of paralysis on the 21st day of September, 1868, in the 84th year of his age.

His remains were interred in the Tomna-hurich Cemetery, where neither stone nor slab marks his grave. If Fearchair's attendant in the Infirmary had made known his dying request previous to his interment, it is very probable that his injunction would have been attended to, and he would then have been buried in Strathconon instead of Tomnahurich, but the attendant failed to make known the Wanderer's request till some time after his demise.

Photographs of Fearchair-a-Ghunna may still be had in Inverness and Dingwall. An oil painting of him, set in a gold-gilt frame, may also be seen at Clachuile Inn, in the parish of Urray. It was taken by a peripatetic limner, and conveys a very good idea of the subject of our sketch. The greatest difficulty was experienced in getting him to "sit" while his photograph was being taken, and the painting seemed at one time to be a hopeless enterprise. Both were, however, ultimately produced, and, as we have said, are good like-nesses.